HAYWARD ANNUAL
1982:
BRITISH DRAWING

HAYWARD GALLERY, LONDON
17 JULY - 30 AUGUST
1982

HAYWARD ANNUAL 1982: BRITISH DRAWING

**SELECTED FROM AN OPEN SUBMISSION
BY KENNETH ARMITAGE, GILLIAN AYRES, FRANCES CAREY,
MARK FRANCIS AND EUAN UGLOW**

Arts Council
OF GREAT BRITAIN

Exhibition organised by Susan Ferleger Brades
assisted by Jocelyn Poulton

Catalogue designed by Richard Hollis
Printed in Great Britain by Graphis Press Limited, London

Copyright © 1982 The Arts Council of Great Britain and the authors

ISBN 0 7287 0324 6

All photographs by Jonathan Bayer
except p.79 by Pru Cuming Associates, p.42 by Paul Wakefield,
p.74 courtesy Ron Haselden and Taylor Nuttall and
p.31 courtesy Patrick Symons

A list of Arts Council publications,
including all exhibition catalogues in print,
can be obtained from
the Publications Officer
Arts Council of Great Britain
105 Piccadilly
London W1V 0AU

CONTENTS

PREFACE

Since the inception of the Hayward Annual exhibitions in 1977, artists and professional colleagues have been urging us to select one of the exhibitions from an open submission. It is with the **Hayward Annual 1982**, the fifth in the series, that we have been able to do this. Coincidentally, the 1982 Annual is also the first to be devoted exclusively to work in one medium: drawing.

The Hayward Annuals aim to present a cumulative picture of contemporary British art as it develops. In that sense, no one annual is itself comprehensive, and the nature of an open submission is such that there are inevitably gaps that would not exist in a differently selected exhibition: artists one might have hoped to include didn't enter; work of merit and interest is rejected due to the limitations of gallery space. For the **Hayward Annual 1982**, 2200 artists from all over the country submitted more than 6000 drawings. The definition of drawing given in our *Notice to Artists* — any kind of drawing that would not otherwise be categorised as a painting, sculpture, print, photograph or performance piece — was deliberately broad in the hope that this would more accurately allow for and attract a range of contemporary work in the medium. Indeed, this drawing exhibition is filled with work that digresses from the notion of drawing as black and white and linear, but we believe it attests to a healthily diverse artistic situation.

It is the members of our selection panel whom we must thank first: Kenneth Armitage, Gillian Ayres, Frances Carey, Mark Francis and Euan Uglow have taken a lively interest in the project from the start. They have helped to shape it throughout and their stamina and concern is everywhere evident. The catalogue introductions have been written by John Elderfield, Director, Department of Drawings and Curator, Department of Painting and Sculpture, at The Museum of Modern Art, New York and by Mark Francis. Both essays focus not on the exhibition but on the meaning and nature of drawing itself.

The administration of the submission was undertaken by Jackie Ford who has also worked with us on the realisation of the exhibition. We are grateful to her and to our handlers Martin Cook, George Gross, David Sims, Carmel Smith and McKenzie Thorpe for their help during the selection process. We would also like to thank the Regional Arts Associations, private dealers and art magazines, too numerous to mention individually, whose help in publicising the submission was very much appreciated. Above all, we would like to thank the artists who responded to our announcement and submitted work. The overall quality of the submission has been much commented upon by those involved in the selection.

Joanna Drew
Director of Art

Andrew Dempsey
Assistant Director for London exhibitions

SELECTORS' STATEMENT

Our purpose was to form an exhibition from over 6000 works submitted by 2200 artists. The primary aim was to search for quality within the immensely varied character of work submitted, and yet, in selecting the exhibition, we had to be aware of the limitations of the gallery space. We had previously agreed on a two stage selection process: the first phase involved using the widest mesh in our net where any interest in a work by a member of the panel of five meant it was retained for further consideration. Phase one also gave us an overall view of the range and diversity of the submission. In phase two, we were able to select the exhibition more precisely, where a majority of three votes secured the work.

We can only say that we did our best. We would like to thank all the artists who responded so well to the idea of an open submission, and also Susan Brades and Jackie Ford for their efficient and cheerful organisation and especially for ensuring the vital flow of works to be seen.

Kenneth Armitage / Gillian Ayres / Frances Carey / Mark Francis / Euan Uglow

JOHN ELDERFIELD

NEW DRAWING: NEW ART

I

From time to time, when the course of art can be observed in the process of diverting itself, flowing into new channels perhaps or beginning at least to trickle out of old and leaky containers, at such moments, earnest and up-to-date writers are apt to start worrying about definitions, determined each and every one of them to be cartographer for the cascading new. It usually happens, however, that when the new does reach cascade proportions it sweeps along with it all the neatly-drawn labels that have been erected along its banks; at very least, they get pretty well dampened in the process, and turn out not to be written in permanent, fast-drying ink after all.

Of all our modern arts, drawing is most resistant to definition. A number of books on drawing offer elaborate classifications of the types and forms and purposes of our elusive art. Some even analyse its components. But faced with the very specific task of saying what actually a drawing is, even A-plus authors either invent artificial and arbitrary solutions or simply ask the question before shrugging their shoulders and walking away. The Museum of Modern Art, adopting the former approach, calls every unique work on paper a drawing. The Arts Council of Great Britain, with wonderfully generous evasiveness, has opted for the latter, telling us (and here I follow their *Notice* to artists who submitted works to this exhibition) that, in effect, a drawing is a work of art that would not otherwise be categorised as a work of art that is not a drawing. This victory of tautology over morphology turns out, in fact, to have produced an extremely interesting and provocative show, and if it includes a number of items that I for one find it very hard to consider drawings, then (as the *Notice to Artists* also says) the intention of the exhibition was to reflect the broad definition of drawing that has characterised contemporary work in the medium. And this it certainly does; and rightly so: had it not, it could hardly have illuminated the state of contemporary art in general in the way that is perhaps the greatest of its fascinations.

Drawing will not be defined; not here, certainly. I too gladly turn my back on the problem. But I do raise it for a very particular and topical reason. A drawing exhibition now (this exhibition, at least) not only reveals but seems actually to embody the central currents of avant-garde art (to use, on purpose, an old and almost anachronistic term) in a way that was not quite the case even a decade ago. By then, to be sure, drawing had noisily pushed itself into the forefront of avant-garde activity, but with few exceptions (and I will return to this later) it achieved its prominence and visibility more because it surrounded the experimental kernel than because it constituted it. Now, however, drawing has worked its way to the centre; to such an extent, indeed, that the new painting in particular defers to what it has to say.

Implicitly at least, the subject of this exhibition is not only new drawing itself but also, in part, a veritable flood of extremely various and often seemingly very eccentric new art that depends on drawing to an extent unusual in recent times (to which dependence its apparent eccentricity is partly to be attributed) — new art that exists, in fact, as securely in the medium of drawing as anywhere else. Drawing that will not be defined is at the centre of new art-making, which itself therefore resists easy definition by virtue of its intimacy with drawing. At which point (having, in any case, already rejected the earnest writers' neatly-drawn labels), we might be forgiven for joining the ranks of those usually but not always elderly writers who are too sure of their positions or too weary of change to want to bother with yet another complication in what had seemed a happily-charted clear course that was plotted long ago. But that won't do either. Whether we like it or not, contemporary art has turned into a muddy torrent of new talent and drawing is somewhere there in the middle of it all. Anyone at all interested in the history of taste, let alone the history of art or the history of drawing, has to be fascinated by what is going on.

II

Most of the drawings in this exhibition are complete and independent works, each secure in its own fictive domain. In saying this, I deliberately avoid the concept of autonomy. Modernism may have produced more autonomous drawings than earlier periods, but drawing's independence from other arts had already long been declared. What was new with modernism, however, was the fictional status that it afforded to this art, as it did to all the other arts it touched. Drawing became self-absorbed. True, a number of drawings in this exhibition were obviously made in that way, honoured by tradition, where the artist's eyes have hardly time to see the sheet, so riveted are they to the scene before him lest it somehow change its appearance while he is not looking. By far the majority, however, whether figurative or abstract, preserve the world only as a distant memory (not necessarily any the less real for that), being constructed, as it were, eyes down, absorbed in what can be solicited from the sheet itself. It may have required the creation of abstract art for this kind of drawing to properly be established, but it persists even without abstraction. Not only does the world, when it is represented, tend often to be a hermetically enclosed one, the drawing that gives it shape is as completely its own and as separate a thing as any modern picture: more in the world, in fact, than of it.

We reach a detour at this point which will take us to the place of volumetric representation in contemporary drawing, and how the artist's eyes pressing against the flat sheet seem to have squeezed volumes virtually out of existence except in a highly schematised form. But that is not where we are going. We are keeping, for the moment, to the fictional independence of drawing . . . which leads us immediately to the way that drawing, fifteen or twenty years ago, appeared to have found for itself an absolute independence, even from picture-making, to such an extent as to have a definable identity of its own. Until fairly recently (until the proliferation, that is, of the extremely various kinds of drawing such as dominate this exhibition; at least, until their public acceptance), 'advanced' drawing tended to operate on the assumption that drawing had become as prescribed a medium as painting, with its own unique norms and conventions. What had happened, in fact, was that advanced drawing (like advanced painting and sculpture) had become a narrowly refined art in which the multiple possibilities and undefinable nature of the medium had been pared down to either the autographically or the diagramatically minimal. It was a movement and not a medium that defined its independence from picture-making (if indeed it did that), and the medium, too tightly compressed too long, sprang back quite sharply, determined to show us all it could really do.

That, at least, in hasty outline, is the linear history of recent drawing. But recent drawing has not, in fact, been confined to a single path, narrow at one moment, broad at the next. While this exhibition does indeed accurately reflect a current and widespread reaction against the more programmatic, reductive, and usually abstract, forms of recent modernism in favour of a more inclusive, eventful, and usually imagist, art, it should not be allowed to persuade us that the inclusiveness it exhibits — let alone the eventfulness and the imagism — is new to recent drawing. Only its popularity is new — one of the special fascinations of the exhibition being the juxtaposition it affords of older and indigenous beside newer and 'international' manifestations of the 'new' art that turns out not to be so new after all. None of which, however, is to deny that it has taken on a highly distinctive character as it has become popular. The character, and burden, assumed by new drawing as drawing has become central to avant-garde experiment in virtually all media is a very distinctive one indeed. Drawing's own innate inclusiveness and lack of definability have become paradigmatic of recent avant-garde art as a whole, which reaches, with the help of drawing, into all sorts of odd corners (a lot of them very dusty, not having been disturbed for a long time) to bring out a whole variety of thought-to-be-lost properties (illustrations, strange materials, naive and fantastic images, faithful and unfaithful portraits, old expressionist prints: things of this kind), many, of course, which turn out to be quite useless and better left alone, but among them a few small treasures, which makes the effort all worthwhile.

III

Less easily-defined media have tended to become foci of avant-garde experimentation. The avant-garde, I know, is now so democratised as hardly to deserve that dashing name but I continue to use it here in order to distinguish a kind of aggressive, expansionist rush to replace the present that opposes not only the conventional but the traditional as well. Since it is tradition that identifies the individual arts, the avant-gardist tends to be attracted to those of them on which tradition has been able to establish less firm a hold: that is to say, to those whose identities are less clearly defined. While the full potential of drawing for avant-garde experimentation had not, until fairly recently, been discovered, its turn has now come. Sculpture, of late another notoriously vague art, had previously held centre-stage in this regard, and before that para-theatrical activity of different kinds. The emergence of drawing as an avant-garde art after having been simply a modernist one for so long (and still continuing to be, of course, in many hands) is a fascinating topic. (We see it, still modest in ambition, waiting in the wings of para-theatre, making plans, diagrams, and so on; gaining in confidence next to sculpture, both of them

11

increasing in size and simplification; then rushing ahead as the avant-garde abandons abstraction; and all the time trying to keep a hold on its purely modernist and pre-modernist past.) But even more fascinating is the way that its very emergence responds to, and reveals, a crisis within modernism itself, as well as in the avant-garde, which thrives on crisis, of course.

This exhibition, I said earlier, is an extremely interesting and provocative one. It admirably fulfills a useful reportorial function as a barometer of the climate of contemporary drawing; and contemporary drawing, it suggests, is in an extremely lively condition. It is also an exhibition that contains what are, to me, a number of highly impressive works as well as a (naturally) larger number of less impressive ones. (Such an imbalance has always characterised every art, and there is no reason to assume that this will change.) What it certainly shows is that drawing, however we choose to define it, is in a more robust and expansive mood — admitting broader and more various kinds of expression — than it has been for some time.

This is not to say, however, that more great drawings are now being made. I very much doubt, in fact, that this is so; for it would be foolish to pretend that we are now in a period of great new art. It seems clear that no truly major new artists have emerged for about twenty years; lacking the impetus and direction that such figures traditionally provide, the visual arts in general have become fragmented, eclectic and confused, so that there now coexists a wide variety of different and competing new trends and an even wider variety of qualitative achievement. If there is any common denominator to be discovered among the newest of the new (and some of the older too), it is the challenge it presents to the narrowness and sophistication (neither term is used disparagingly) of recent modernism, and the attempt to graft a more vigourous stock onto a mainstream that has grown, in some hands, thin and sickly through overcultivation. The green thumb of genius would seem to be required for grafts of this kind to properly take, and this has not yet appeared; but in the meantime, gregarious drawing is attracting most of those who seem determined to break with recent modernism: often through that searching, to which I referred earlier, into the rougher corners of the art-historical past, as well as of the vernacular present. Renewal, it seems, always begins in regression. The impetus of modernism having apparently faltered and the avant-garde exhausted its extremist possiblities, drawing happily opens the atavistic door that leads hopefully to fresh beginnings. It is a kind of remedial regression that is being attempted, through which art, ideally at least, is to be restored to a state of primitive grace.

IV

Whether or not our visual arts are in the turbulent process of cultural change of the most radical kind is still too early to tell, for out of today's roughcast Rousseauism has not yet come anything of overpowering quality, though much that is strong and lively as well as much that is merely loud. Moreover, what is happening now is not entirely without precedent in earlier modernism. Twice before (in the eighteen nineties and the nineteen thirties) it seemed as if modernism was in danger of replacement, with no major new talent appearing, which produced periods of eclecticism and turbulence similar to that which exists now. Twice before, modernism survived, and among the lessons to be learned from its survival is the following:

At moments of crisis in modernism, when painting, the pioneering modernist art, loses its pictorially innovating thrust, it tends to look outside of its own normative possibilities, turning to things literary and illustrational for iconographical help and to other and related media for formal enrichment. At such moments, the very inclusiveness of drawing turns out to be a good source of fringe benefits, being able to feed into the mainstream of advanced art, whenever it becomes narrow and attenuated, new sources, new subjects, new formal possibilities; also, new awareness of its origins in direct and spontaneous inscription. This, in its turn, brings drawing itself into new prominence. The result, at least immediately, does tend to be a somewhat lesser art (for the greatest monuments of Western culture do seem to be produced, experience tells us, not during but after revisions of this kind); also, a somewhat eclectic one, as if the loss of faith in historically transmitted authority (which called for revision) is reflected in the very discontinuity of the work produced. There are obvious dangers here: most obviously, perhaps, that the kind of unity such art does offer is a merely compensatory unity (compensatory, that is, of the discontinuity with tradition that it expresses). In those earlier moments of modernist crisis, that danger was eventually surpassed, and out of it, in both cases, did come renewal, and renewal of the most wonderful and surprising kind. Whether this will happen now is still, as I say, too early to tell. And whether this will happen because of, or despite, the kind of new works that dominate this exhibition is also too early to tell.

What can reasonably be told is that our current moment is far from being dull. Art in general, and drawing in particular, may not be the pure and perfect thing that it once was. But it turns out to be in far more intriguing a position than it was even in those previous moments of modernist revision; certainly far more extreme in its contrasts of good and bad, and awaiting, I suspect (and hope), far more extreme contrasts yet.

MARK FRANCIS

THE DIFFICULTIES AND PLEASURES OF DRAWING

'Ce dessin me plait'
MATISSE, 1945

Drawing is infinitely mysterious, and at the same time mundane. To start with, we make marks — only subsequently can we distinguish graphically between writing and drawing. In the end, the best draughtsmen can perform the 'miraculous' feat of turning what is technically and imaginatively difficult into something direct, simple, and quick. Drawing contains paradoxes: a single line can express volume and space, light is suggested by the paper which is left untouched. Symbols, numbers, or other notations reside as the trace of human thought and movements. The fleeting or exploratory character of many drawings is often the result, however, of intense concentration, and of long training or apprenticeship.

It can be profoundly disturbing to see photographs of the apparently misanthropic frown on Matisse's face as he worked on his casual, languorous and erotic drawings. His ability to leave only the minimum necessary trace, sufficient to make manifest the desired image, had clearly been acquired by discipline and experience, but the lines on the paper still appear as if by a natural order. 'Ce dessin me plait': this phrase is written on his tiny sketch of a woman looking at an unmarked sheet of paper, itself indicated only by a simple outline.[1] This bagatelle was composed in Matisse's last years, during the period in which he discovered the pleasures of his late paper cut-outs, the most purely hedonistic and joyful 'drawings' of our century. The written words become an expression of pleasure, uttered by the figure in the drawing (and by Matisse himself) which cannot be completely conveyed in the lines of the image itself. The physical act of drawing and the creation of the image can be pleasurable in themselves, and this is indeed recognised in some therapeutic uses of drawing. But for the artist both the image and the making of it are difficult.

In drawing, as in painting and sculpture, a period of systematic exploration and analysis has yielded recently to a greater freedom of technique and of subject. During the latter half of the 1960s and '70s, many of the most radical artists, both in Britain and abroad, concentrated their attention on single aspects of the language of art to produce work which would be more refined, more direct, or more far-reaching than had been considered appropriate before. The materials and techniques of drawing naturally became a part of this analysis. It was possible for Philip Rawson to write in the preface to his book Drawing (published 1969) that 'there are no accepted names for the facts of artistic execution as there are for the facts of musical language'. Rawson's book describes an awesome range of materials, surfaces and supports, iconographical references, and so on. Quite apart from showing how few drawings are 'finished' drawings as such, he demonstrates how restricted is the modern European idea of what a drawing may be. Within the world of art — as distinct from, say, graffiti on the streets — the narrow scope of the capacity and resources of drawing has to some extent recently been enlarged.

At the end of the 1960s, the boundaries of 'drawing' were being extended in this country by, to take only two examples, Hamish Fulton in *The Sweet Grass Hills of Montana* (1971), a small book in which a brushed image of a mountain is redrawn on each successive page from the memory of the preceding one, and by Gilbert and George in their remarkable series of huge pencil drawings depicting the artists in the landscape. Developments such as these were surveyed internationally in two important exhibitions later in the decade, *Functions of Drawing* at the Kröller-Müller Museum in Otterlo, Holland (1975) and *Drawing Now* at The Museum of Modern Art, New York (1976). Despite these attempts, we have come no nearer to an adequate taxonomy of drawing in the last decade. This may not be a bad thing. Certainly it will take more time for drawing to be properly regarded as a purposeful and self-sufficient activity. Even now wholly unnecessary distinctions of quality or meaning are generally made between drawings made by 'professional' artists, by students (whether of art, design, architecture, etc.), by children, or by those employing them as part of various kinds of therapy. The terms of reference are still too vague, or half-understood, to begin a fruitful discourse.

That said, it is worth noting at least one significant line of enquiry which has renewed itself in this country since the mid-1970s. A watershed was marked by Kitaj's exhibition *The Human Clay* in 1977. At the time it was taken to signify a return to 'academic' values, the apprenticeship of the life-class and the primacy of the single human figure as a subject. But this would be to restrict the power of that exhibition as an index of changes occurring in various ways throughout the art world, and would also obscure the history of that generation of British artists to which Kitaj belongs. Certainly the mesmerising intensity of Auerbach's drawings comes from their unsparing examination of a single human figure alone with the artist, but Kitaj's most powerful drawings are made not only from life, but also from the collage devices he has developed at the same time in his paintings, which at their best bring together disparate images into a new relationship charged with symbolic force. Terry Atkinson, Colin Self, or Peter Sylveire, who were contemporaries at the Slade at the same time as Kitaj and Hockney were at the Royal College, have also been able to incorporate diverse cultural and historical references in an art which is only residually indebted to academic conventions. In the current enthusiasm for revision of the post-war history of British art, it would therefore be misleading to believe in the benefits of a wholesale return to traditional values and working methods, without denying the seminal importance of those artists (often born in the war years or immediately afterwards) who went to art school in the early 1960s, and who have given their academic training a radical overhaul. But there are other kinds of drawings which seem to have disappeared, or not yet to have made an appearance in Britain. Perhaps there is always a temptation in surveys which are restricted to the art of one country, to search for shared cultural characteristics which may be apparent or absent. While it may be possible, for instance, to trace a figurative tradition in England, one could as easily regret the apparent decline of the caricature and the grotesque from the vigorous lines of Hogarth and Rowlandson.

Historically there seems to have been a dichotomy established between the 'expressive' and the 'precise' in drawing. Technical drawings, or working drawings for sculpture, for instance, are believed to be precise, 'economic', and thereby to evince a kind of rational truth. Expressive drawing,

16

on the other hand, is loose, or 'spendthrift', having a kind of emotional authenticity made evident by the traces of the artist's hand. A resolution of these positions may be seen in the drawings and paintings of the American Cy Twombly, which retain a hermetic, private quality while at the same time professing the tone of a public utterance. His work combines the appearance of extreme elegance with a crude and hesitant manner, so that the evanescent, fleeting quality of spontaneity (as in the art of children, or of graffiti) is retained in an art which is refined and elusive. Vestigial images and writing, the erotic and the violent, classical mythology and personal autobiography, all these are traced in Twombly's fragmentary and evocative pictures. His *style* is impossible to imitate, but as Roland Barthes writes in the essay 'The Wisdom of Art', the desire wells up in the spectator to share the experience of the artist: 'Thus this morning of 31 December 1978, it is still dark, it is raining, all is silent when I sit down again at my worktable. I look at [Twombly's] *Hérodiade* and I have really nothing to say about it except the same platitude: that I like it [*que ça me plaît!*]. But suddenly there arises something new, a desire: that of *doing the same thing*; of going to another worktable (no longer that for writing), to choose colours, to paint and draw'.[2]

1. Catalogue, Galerie Maeght, Paris, 1945
2. Roland Barthes, 'The Wisdom of Art' in *Cy Twombly: Paintings and Drawings 1954-77*,
   Whitney Museum of American Art, New York, 1979

ARTISTS IN THE EXHIBITION

One work by each artist is reproduced
on the page number shown

20

EXPLANATORY NOTE

The catalogue is arranged in broadly chronological order based on the year of artists' births. One work by every artist selected for the exhibition is illustrated. Additional work by an artist that has been selected for the exhibition is also listed. Although it may not be possible to hang all works put forward by the selection panel for the exhibition, at least one work by every artist chosen is included in the exhibition. Unless otherwise stated, works are on paper and in the collection of the artist. Dimensions are given in inches, height precedes width followed, when relevant, by depth. A number of works in the exhibition are for sale; information can be obtained from the ticket desk at the Hayward Gallery or from the Exhibition Organiser, Arts Council of Great Britain, 105 Piccadilly, London W1V 0AU.

An alphabetical list of artists in the exhibition, with the page number on which their work appears, can be found on pp.19-21.

HENRY MUNDY
b.1919

UNTITLED
1982
Mixed media
20x29

Also selected:

UNTITLED
1982
Mixed media
26x36

UNTITLED
1982
Mixed media
26x36

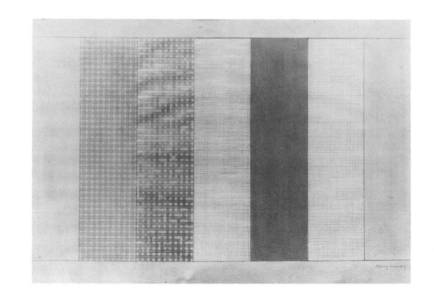

CLARENCE BLACKBURN
b.1914

ASPECTS OF HMS VICTORY
IN DRY DOCK AT PORTSMOUTH
1976
Watercolour drawing with pen work
31x43

24

DENIS COOPER-KING
b.1919

A NIGHT SCENE
October 1981
Charcoal
25¼ x 35½

ADRIAN HEATH
b.1920

STUDY
1980
Pencil and chalk
30x22

Also selected:

STUDY
1982
Pencil and wash
10x9½

STUDY
1982
Pencil and chalk
10x9½

25

MAURICE SUMRAY
b.1920

FIRST DRAFT FOR THE PAINTING
APPLE GATHERERS
1981
Pencil
16½ x 13½

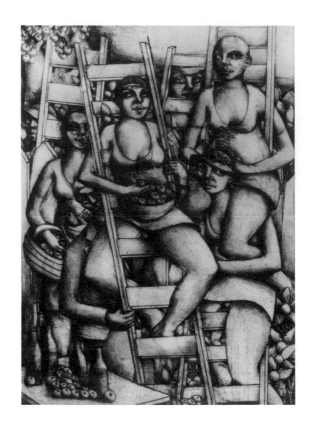

ROBERT ROSE
b.1920

LIFE DRAWING 2
1982
Pencil
15 x 19½

PETER DE FRANCIA
b.1921

FIGURES IN A GARDEN
1979
Charcoal
19½ x 24¾

Also selected:

MINOTAUR
1980
Charcoal
21¾ x 29¾

RICHARD YOUNG
b.1921

INTERIOR L8
1979
Chalk
15 x 10

27

ALBERT IRVIN
b.1922

ALBA
1982
Watercolour and gouache
63x52

CHRISTOPHER PEMBERTON
b.1923

CARNEVILLE: LANDSCAPE
1979
Pencil
14x22

28

JEFFERY CAMP
b.1923

HANG GLIDERS BEACHY HEAD
1982
Charcoal
24½ x34

Also selected:

MAGPIES BEACHY HEAD
1982
Conté and Chinese Ink
22½ x22½

YOUNG AND OLD
AT BEACHY HEAD
1982
Pastel and pencil
26x20

ANTHONY EYTON
b.1923

BENARES
1982
Pastel and charcoal
40x54
Browse and Darby Ltd

Also selected:

CAMBERWELL CANTEEN
1982
Pastel
24¾x30
Browse and Darby Ltd

30

GERI MORGAN
b.1926

PABLO CONDELUCCI
1981
Pencil
18x15

PATRICK SYMONS
b.1925

COWS
1977-81
Charcoal
25¾x37
Browse and Darby Ltd

CONSTANCE STUBBS
b.1927

ADDICTION
JUST ONE MORE TIME
1982
Charcoal
36x25

JEAN-MARY CARTWRIGHT
b.1928

BREAKFAST
Summer 1980
Pastel
24x21½

32

VICTOR WILLING
b.1928

26.10.81
1981
Charcoal and pastel
15⅛ x11¼

Also selected:

8.3.81
1981
Charcoal and pastel
14x19¼

KATHLEEN HYNDMAN

STUDY FOR SOFT SWELL
SIDMOUTH I
February 1982
Pencil
22x30

33

DAVE GILBERT
b.1928

GHOST OF THE MOUNTAIN
HARE NO.1
1982
Charcoal
11¾x16½

Also selected:

EARLY WARNING SYSTEM
NO.2
1980
Charcoal
7x5

EVEN HERE IN OUR EXILE NO.5
1981
Charcoal
11¾x16½

ADRIAN BERG
b.1929

CHISWICK HOUSE
1978
Pen
18½ x 17¼
Lent by the artist;
courtesy Waddington Galleries

ROY OXLADE
b.1929

WOMAN ON CHAIR
1978
Charcoal
33 x 23½

35

EVELYN WILLIAMS
b.1929

THE ATTIC ROOM
1977
Charcoal
31x53

MICHAEL KELLAWAY
b.1929

LIZ. VERSION III
1977
Pencil
69x30

RICHARD BLOMFIELD
b.1930

SEASCAPE: ARBROATH
1981
Pencil and crayon
8¾x12½

ASSHETON GORTON
b.1930

WORKING DRAWING FOR
LAPUTA, GULLIVER'S TRAVELS
1981
Pencil
92x192

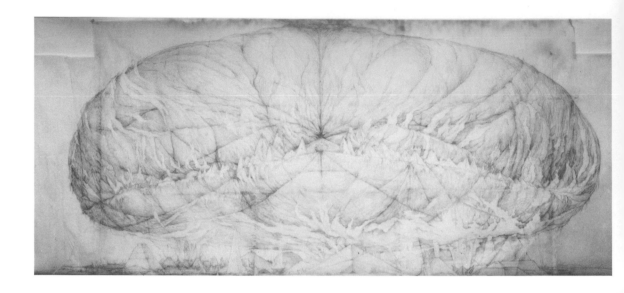

MARC SEWELL
b.1930

DRAWING FOR SCULPTURE
September 1981
Charcoal and chalk
31x21

38

GERALD JARMAN
b.1930

LOWERING A SOLDIER FROM
A TRENCH PARAPET
(FIGURES DERIVED FROM
THE ENTOMBMENT,
MICHELANGELO,
NATIONAL GALLERY,
LONDON)
1982
Pencil
40x27

Also selected:

A SOLDIER
1981
Pencil
21x55

39

ANTHONY WHISHAW
b.1930

TOWARDS STOWTING
1981-82
Crayon, pastel, ash,
charcoal, acrylic and wash
77x192
Lent by the artist;
courtesy of Nicola Jacobs Gallery

JOHN EMANUEL
b.1930

STANDING FIGURE
1981
Charcoal
31½ x 22½

PETER DAGLISH
b.1930

AMBUSH
1978
Charcoal
41 x 27½

41

LEONARD McCOMB
b.1930

PORTRAIT OF LOUISE ARNOLD
1980
Pencil
55x31½

Also selected:

PORTRAIT OF PIPPA WILDE,
ROYAL BALLET
1980
Pencil
64x31½

PORTRAIT OF MARIANNE
SUNDER
1981
Pencil and watercolour
69x46

42

GEORGE WILSON
b.1930

SHELTER
April 1980
Charcoal
18¾ x 28¾

NATALIE DOWER
b.1931

WORKING DRAWING,
DODECAGON
1982
Pencil and acrylic
14¼ x 14¼

Also selected:

WORKING DRAWING,
DOUBLE SQUARE
1981
Pencil and acrylic
14¼ x 24½

43

ELISABETH FRINK
b.1930

SEATED MAN
1982
Pencil
39x28
Lent by the artist;
courtesy Waddington Galleries

TOM ESPLEY
b.1931

STILL LIFE, MANTEL PIECE
1979
Charcoal
23x30¼

NOEL FORSTER
b.1932

UNTITLED
1982
Acrylic on brown paper
with grey and white inserts
17x24

Also selected:

UNTITLED
1982
Acrylic on white paper
with brown and grey inserts
18½x23¾

DENNIS CREFFIELD
b.1931

THE LIGHTHOUSE
AT KATO PAPHOS,
CYPRUS
1981
Charcoal
33x23

46

SONIA LAWSON
b.1934

WEDDING
1982
Chalk and ink on canvas
50x40

Also selected:

HOMAGE TO MOLIÈRE
AND WATTEAU
1981
Chalk and ink on canvas
50x40

MOORLAND BENEDICTION
1981
Chalk, ink and paper on canvas
44½ x36

47

JOHN LYONS
b.1933

LOVERS
1981
Pen, ink and graphite
17x13

JOHN LEWIS
b.1933

SUMMER LANDSCAPE
1981
Charcoal
28½x21

48

STASS PARASKOS
b.1933

RUINS
1982
Conté on card
18x25

VICTOR WILLIS
b.1934

MIDSUMMER NIGHT'S DREAM
(DRAWING FOR PAINTING)
1982
Charcoal
15½x22

BASIL BEATTIE
b.1935

BLACK LIGHT
1982
Oil and collage
52x38½

Also selected:

GREEN VEE
July 1981
Oil
54x40
Collection of Lyn Gambles

BRIAN PEACOCK
b.1935

GARDEN, SHADOWS
January 1982
Charcoal
35x35

50

PAULA REGO
b.1935

RABBIT AND WEEPING CABBAGE
1982
Acrylic
36x48

Also selected:

MONKEY DRAWING
1981
Acrylic
30x22
Edward Totah Gallery

51

ROSE WYLIE
b.1934

BOY MEETS GIRL
January 1982
Pencil
30x22

DOUGLAS ABERCROMBIE
b.1934

SAND DRAWING I
1981
Sand on canvas
62x98

VICTOR NEWSOME
b.1935

UNTITLED — 1980
(HEAD C)
1980
Ink and pencil
12⅝ x16½
Private collection

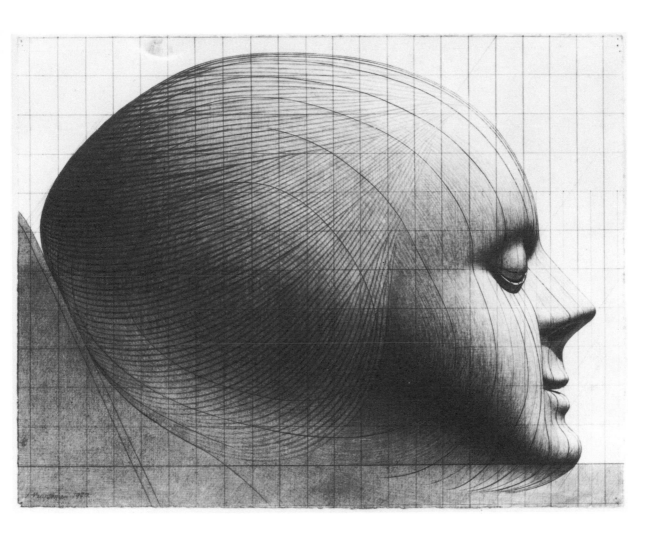

BRYAN TAYLOR
b.1935

THE BURRANO VALLEY, ITALY
NO.1
1976
Charcoal
28x36

MAURICE COCKRILL
b.1936

MARTYRDOM
1982
Charcoal
54x40

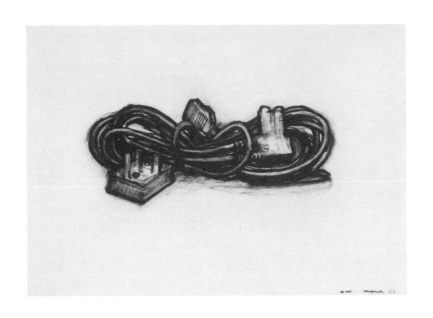

ALAN WELSFORD
b.1936

LEADS
March 1981
Conté
16½ x 23⅜

FRANCIS WEST
b.1936

THE INTERLUDE
1981
Pencil
40x48

HARRY ABEND
b.1937

LENU-LENU
1981
Oil stick
48x95½

ALLEN JONES
b.1937

MAIN LINE/
FOGAL MURAL PROJECT
December 1980
Pencil and oleopasto
5x13

56

RAYMOND ATKINS
b.1937

LOUISE GRAHAM LEANING
BACKWARD
1979
Pencil, coloured pencil and
oil pastel
30x22
John Winstone

SARGY MANN
b.1937

HOME
1982
Compressed charcoal
60x79½

57

TOM PHILLIPS
b.1937

SONATA: TRIPTYCH
1981
Chalk and pastel
3 sections, each 48x30
Lent by the artist;
courtesy Waddington Galleries

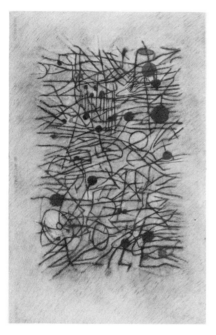 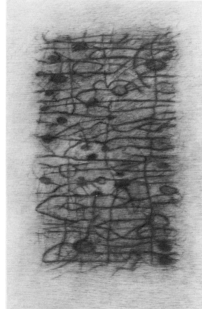 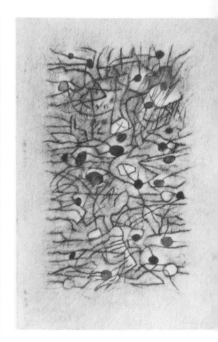

DAVID LEVERETT
b.1938

VIEWS FROM
THE CITADELS SERIES;
RECENT VIEWS OF
DISTANT PLACES
MNEMONIC PIECES
1981-82
Ink and paint
31½ x 47

WYNN JONES
b.1939

FALLING AND CRAWLING
1981
Charcoal and pastel
14¾ x 20½

59

KATE WESTBROOK

AUNT MARJORIE (1902-1979)
VISITING CRETE
1979
Oil pastel on paper
16¾ x 13¾

IAN HUNTER
b.1939

THE MARRIAGE BED II
February 1982
Charcoal
27x40

Also selected:

THE MARRIAGE BED III
February 1982
Charcoal
27x40

TERRY ATKINSON
b.1939

THE BLACK ART OF
PROLETARIAN GOB-EATING 4:
PRIVATE PINEAPPLE-ROMANOFF,
WURTEMBURG INFANTRYMAN,
NR. AMIENS, JULY 1918
1980
Chalk, gouache and pencil
59x44

Also selected:

NON IDEOLOGICAL
CAMOUFLAGE,
IDEOLOGICAL SKY
1980

or
(Title 2:)
TITLE: UNTITLED
or
(Title 3:)
SHAPE DRAWING EXERCISE —
'CLEARLY THIS ARTIST HAS NOT
BEEN TRAINED WELL IN THE FINE ART
OF DRAWING SHAPES'.
or
(Title 4:)
INSTRUCTION FROM A BOURGEOIS
LIBERAL SPECTATOR.

Instruction:
    "Leave the picture untitled, this allows the spectator more scope for free association and thereby accords more with the democratic aspirations of bourgeois liberal freedoms?"
Question:
    "Can we, therefore, deduce from this comment of yours that abstract work is the most historically developed and appropriate art of and to bourgeois liberal democracy?"
Answer:
    "I'm not sure about that, but of one thing I am sure. I am a person of moderation, balance and the radical centre and from this most clear-viewed and reasonable of positions I can see that there is something not to be trusted about this artist raising these issues in this kind of way. I think he's probably a Trotskyist, you know, a member of the 'Fascist Left'."
Question:
    "But surely 'Fascist Left' is a historical contradiction and...?"
Answer:
    "Shut up, I know what Fascism is, after all I'm a person of moderation."
Question:
    "But.....?"
Answer:
    "Shut up and listen.....".'
                    Conté
                    68x104

MEDIANIK 4:
THE NEWSCASTER ENTOMBED BY
THE NEWS
1982
Chalk and pencil
22x30

61

JOHN LESSORE
b.1939

PAULE AT KAYMOS
1981
Pencil and black ink
6½x8

ANDREW RYDER
b.1939

APPROACHING THE PRIMITIVE
February 1982
Oil pastel, coloured pencil, conté
and feathers on heavy brown paper
with brass eyelets
41⅝x45⅝

JANE BOND
b.1939

MY MOTHER
1979
Charcoal
19x27½

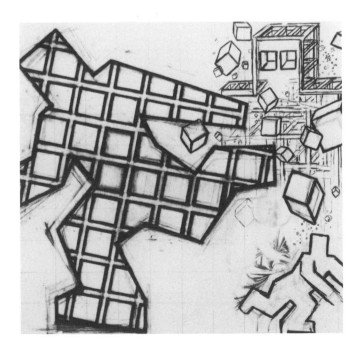

MICHAEL SIMPSON
b.1940

DRAWING FOR
THE RUNNING MAN
January 1982
Chalk and charcoal
60x63

63

MOICH ABRAHAMS
b.1941

HANGING SUBJECT
1981
Pastel
22x19

GEORGE ROWLETT
b.1941

HEAD OF MARION II
1981
Compressed charcoal
22x15

64

LAETITIA YHAP
b.1941

MARK PAINTING UP THE BOAT
AND SMOKY
1981-82
Graphite lead pencil and oil pastel
on paper primed with liquitex
14½ x 17½

Also selected:

WORKSHEET FOR
*PAUL HELPING DOUG AND
SCOBY*
1979
Graphite on envelopes
48 x 18

BOY TOSSING WATER
OVER HIS ROWBOAT
1981
Graphite lead pencil and oil pastel
on paper primed with liquitex
11½ x 16½

BARRY FLANAGAN
b.1941

11.44.50 JULY 29/81
July 1981
Pencil
9⅝ x7¾

Also selected:

A GOLDEN ARROW
1981
Pencil
9⅝ x7¾

MICHAEL KENNY
b.1941

STRANGE OBJECTS IV
1982
Pencil, charcoal, paint
and collage
40x53

66

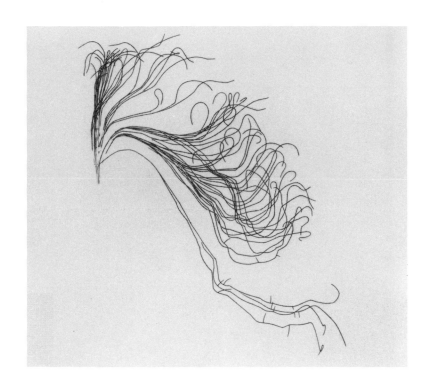

TERENCE HAMMILL
b.1941

ASPARAGUS FERN:
GROWTH IN 66 STAGES
12 March - 9 April 1981
Charcoal
44x50

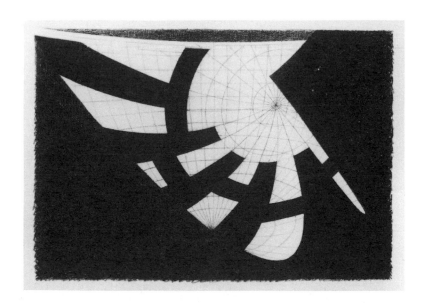

JOHN MAINE
b.1942

JAI PRAKASA YANTRA
1982
Conté
22x31

67

JANE NEARN
b.1942

REALITY
August 1981
Charcoal
32½ x 22½

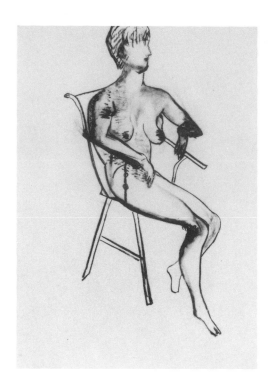

INGRID KERMA
b.1942

AFTERMATH
OR
THE CRABS ARE COMING
1982
Chalk and charcoal
57½ x 48

68

ANA MARIA PACHECO
b.1943

THE RISE AND FALL
OF A TYRANT II
January 1982
Graphite and charcoal
72x72

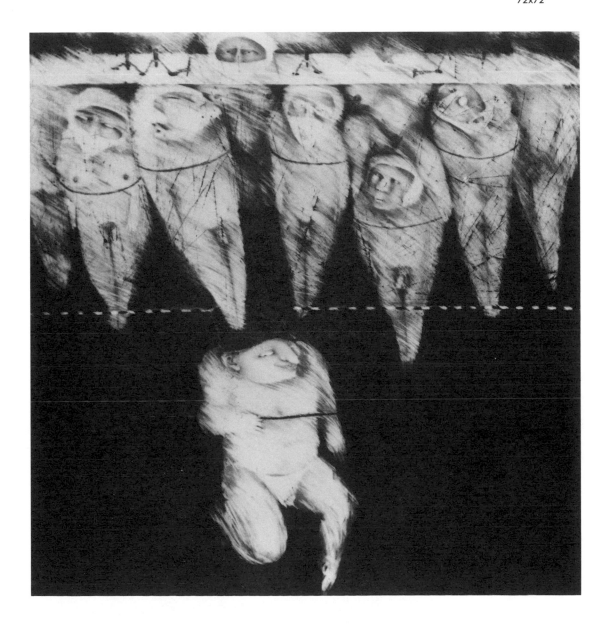

ROY BURDETT
b.1943

HENRY 1981
1981
Charcoal
34½ x 23

GEOFF RIGDEN
b.1943

COAST NEAR FONTANA
AMOROSA, CYPRUS (VIII)
August 1977
Poster colour
15 x 18½

Also selected:

LANDSCAPE, CYPRUS
1977
Conté
19 x 13

70

ROBERT JONES
b.1943

MR. PUNCH BEATS JUDY
1977
Pencil
16x15½

MICHAEL DAVIS
b.1943

UNTITLED
December 1981
Charcoal and conté
32x41½

Also selected:

UNTITLED
March 1982
Charcoal and conté
32x41½

TONY CARTER
b.1943

REMEMBERING LANDSCAPE
1977
Ordnance survey map with
gouache and pencil
26⅜ x21½

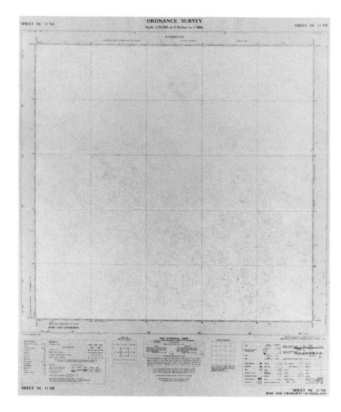

DOUGLAS JEAL
b.1944

KITE
1982
Graphite and coloured pencil
on plastic
28x27¼

Also selected:

SECATEUR DRAWING
1982
Graphite on plastic
14¾ x10½ x8¾

72

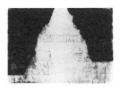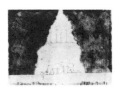

CARL PLACKMAN
b.1943

COEXISTENCE (TRIPTYCH)
1982
Charcoal and gouache
3 sections, each 26¼ x 35½

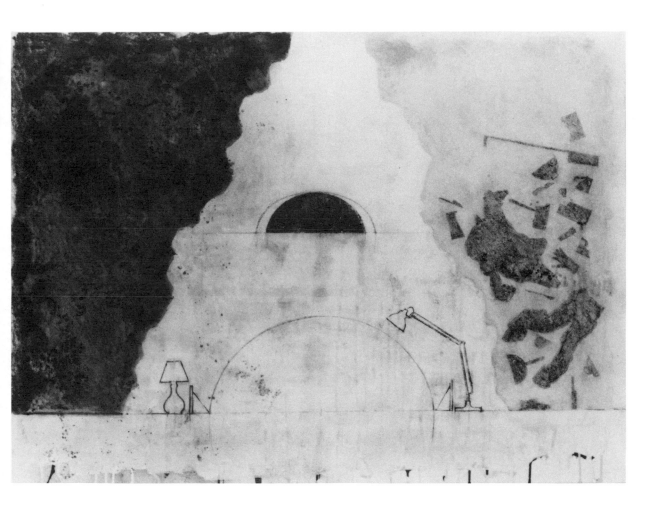

RON HASELDEN
b.1944
AND
TAYLOR NUTTALL
b.1962

HERTFORD UNION
PLAN B
1982
A large-scale work
built on site. This involves non-
collaboration between the artists:
two independent ideas, without
prior discussion, colliding or
interphasing on the same site using
similar material — damaged
scaffolding.

Reproduced but
not in exhibition:

RON HASELDEN

TOWER OF BABEL
1980
Thornhill School,
Sunderland

TAYLOR NUTTALL

STRING CUBE
February 1982

String and nails
on 2D ground
Approx 72x72

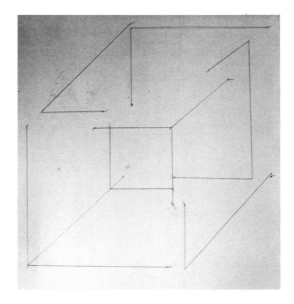

MARTIN NAYLOR
b.1944

MUTÁTIS MUTANTIS NO.2
1977
Wood, acrylic, ink and crayon
120x120
Juda Rowan Gallery

PHILIP O'REILLY
b.1944

STONE CARVER'S STONE
1980
Ink
25¾x17½

75

KEITH BURGESS
b.1944

FIGURES III
June 1981
Pencil
17¼ x 22¼

RODERIC HILL
b.1944

PORTRAIT OF A LADY
1979
Charcoal and chalk
22¾ x 30¾

PHILL ROOKE
b.1944

WORKING ON DRILL CASINGS
(DRAWING FOR SCULPTURE)
April 1981
Pencil
17½ x 16½

DAVID HARDING
b.1944

MOUNTAIN II
1982
Oil pastel
8x6½

Also selected:

MOUNTAIN III
1982
Oil pastel
8x6½

KEITH MILOW
b.1945

UNTITLED
1981
Oil
4 sections, each 38x50
Lent by the artist;
courtesy Waddington Galleries

DAVID TREMLETT
b.1945

AFRICA GIRL
1980
Conté
4 sections, each 22¼ x 30⅛
Lent by the artist;
courtesy Waddington Galleries

DAVID HEPHER
b.1945

VINE
1980
Pencil
25½ x 19½
Angela Flowers Gallery

KEN HENDERSON
b.1945

BATHER
1982
Mixed media
40x50

DAVID SHUTT
b.1945

HALF FIGURE
1980
Pencil
23¼ x 16½

ERICA CUMMING
b.1945

PREGNANT WOMAN
1980
Charcoal
42x27

81

SAM TANNER
b.1945

UNTITLED
March 1980
Charcoal
11x9

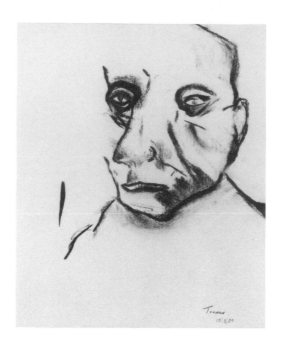

SEBASTIAN VERNEY
b.1945

INNER ADVENTURE
1977
Charcoal
52x58

82

TREVOR FELCEY
b.1945

RICHMOND OAK
1979
Charcoal
27x36
Susan E. Isserlis

ADRIAN HEMMING
b.1945

AEGINA
1981
Charcoal
20x27½

83

DAVID NASH
b.1945

A FALLEN TREE
ALONG A HEDGE
ON A SLOPE
1982
Earth, clay, peat, charcoal and
chalk
on Hayward Gallery wall

BRIAN COLLIER
b.1945

STRATA II
1981
Pencil, graphite and watercolour
on board
29x43

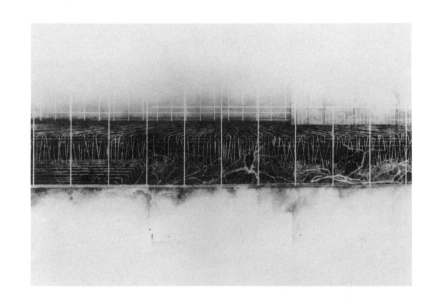

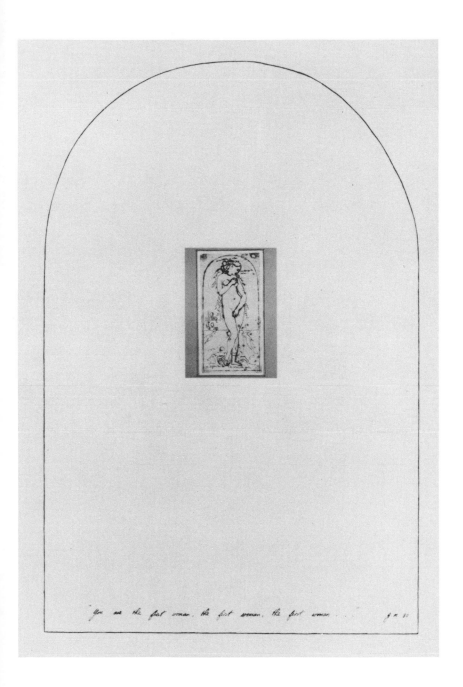

"You are the first woman, the first woman, the first woman..." *J.M. 80*

JOHN MURPHY
b.1945

"YOU ARE
THE FIRST WOMAN,
THE FIRST WOMAN,
THE FIRST WOMAN..."
1980
Postcard, pen and ink
28x19

Also selected:

AFTER
GIULIO ROMANO —
AFTER
JEAN DOMINIQUE
INGRES —
THE PHILOSOPHY
OF TIME
1979
Pencil
29x21

ANTHONY FARRELL
b.1945

HEAD OF SID MEERLOO
1979-80
Pencil
22x16½

ALAN JOHNSTON
b.1945

UNTITLED
1981
Pencil, acrylic and oil
on canvas
84x20

Also selected:

UNTITLED
1981
Pencil, acrylic and oil
on canvas
84x20

86

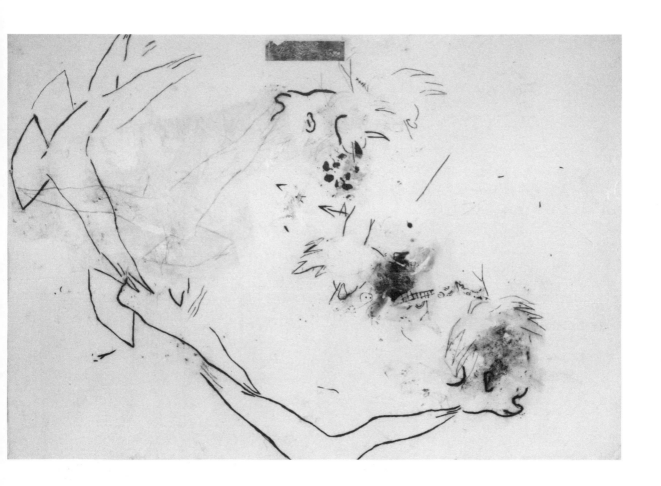

GARY WRAGG
b.1946

FAIR COMPLEXION
February 1982
Charcoal and oil pastel
60x50

Also selected:

UNTITLED
March 1982
Charcoal and oil paint
56x46

SALLY HARGREAVES
b.1946

FIELDS, YAXLEY
1982
Charcoal
15x22

Also selected:

BLACK FIELD, YAXLEY
1982
Charcoal
15x22

BRICKWORKS, YAXLEY
1982
Charcoal and crayon
15x22

STEPHEN YOUNG
b.1946

COUPLE
January 1982
Pastel and charcoal
32x23½

TIMOTHY HYMAN
b.1946

STUDY FOR
SITTING FOR CHRISTOPHER
1979
Pencil
8½x11
Blond Fine Art

DEREK STOCKLEY
b.1946

ABSTRACT I
1981
Wax crayon, watercolour
and coloured ink
32x24

EILEEN LAWRENCE
b.1946

PRAYER STICK
1982
Watercolour
96x6

90

KERRY TRENGOVE
b.1946

ENCLOSURES
November 1981
Intaglio
40x30
Courtesy of the
Lewis Johnstone Gallery

RONALD BOYD
b.1946

LANDSCAPE — AUTUMN
1981
Pencil
12x16

91

PAUL NORTON
b.1946

SELF PORTRAIT
August 1981
Charcoal
24x18½

PETER ARCHER
b.1946

ANGELA RESTING
1980
Conté
15x22

ROBERT MASON
b.1946

STILL LIFE I
(PESCALIA)
1982
Watercolour, charcoal, crayon
and Rhoplex
12x11⅜
Lent by the artist;
courtesy of Anne Berthoud Gallery

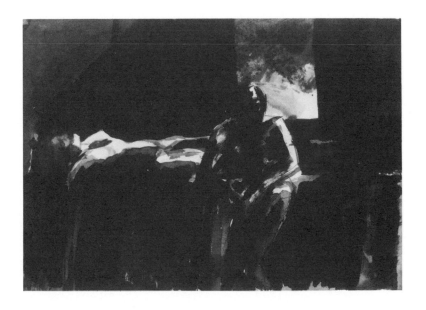

SOTIRAKIS CHARALAMBOU
b.1947

DRAWING IN
CHINESE INK
March 1981
Chinese ink
11 ½ x16 ¼

DAVID WALKER-BARKER
b.1947

LANDSCAPED GARDEN
WITH STONES
January 1982
Pencil, charcoal, oil paint
and coloured pencil
10¼ x 10¼

HARRY BARNETT
b.1947

LOOKING EAST
1982
Pastel and charcoal
60x96

94

PETER BUNTING
b.1947

MAN IN A BROWN STUDY
1981
Oil pastel and crayon
33x23½

NICHOLAS HACKING
b.1947

DOWN TO THE RAILWAY —
MAYFIELD
1981
Charcoal and acrylic on canvas
26x40

Also selected:

MISS Y
1982
Charcoal and acrylic
on canvas
31¾x40

95

ROBIN KLASSNIK
b.1947

WORK
1982
Ink
23x15⅜

SUSAN ENGLEDOW
b.1947

DRAWING OF ANNA
September 1981
Pencil
12x11

96

PETER SEDDON
b.1947

HIGHLAND CLEARANCE
DRAWING NO.1
1981
Pastel
60x60

Also selected:

HIGHLAND CLEARANCE
DRAWING NO.3
1982
Pastel
60x60

97

KEN OLIVER
b.1948

CROSS
December 1981
Acrylic, wax and collage
15x15
Lent by the artist;
courtesy Moira Kelly Fine Art

Also selected:

STREET PARTY
January 1982
Acrylic, wax and collage
15x15
Lent by the artist;
courtesy Moira Kelly Fine Art

STUART KNOWLES
b.1948

KABUKI I, II, III
1982
Mixed media
3 sections, each 60x48

98

JOHN O'DONNELL
b.1948

PORTRAIT OF TOSHO
1978
Charcoal
20x29¼

Also selected:

THE SUNDERLAND
LEAVING WAPPING
May 1980
Caran D'Ache and charcoal
21½x29½

SYLVIA FINZI
b.1948

UNTITLED
1982
Conté
20⅝x15⅝

99

TAKASHI SUZUKI
b.1948

ROOTS AND WINGS
February 1982
Pastel
2 sections, each 22x22

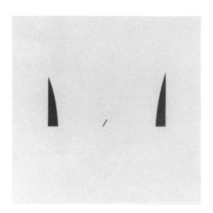

PHILIP STEVENS
b.1948

BIRDSONG
January 1982
Solder drawn on curled support
of metal foil
34½x11x2

100

JERRY COLEMAN
b.1948

STILL LIFE WITH FLY
1981
Pastel
34½ x25

MARIA CHEVSKA
b.1948

ARK (VII) SLIGHTLY PISSED
1982
Charcoal and oil pastel
33x23

101

PAUL ROSENBLOOM
b.1949

WOODCARVER
1981
Pastel
24x17¾
Lent by the artist;
courtesy Nicola Jacobs Gallery

Also selected:

GLIDER
1981
Pastel
17¾x24
Lent by the artist;
courtesy Nicola Jacobs Gallery

DAVID WISEMAN
b.1949

IN TOR WOOD
1982
Charcoal
20x27

102

JOHN STEZAKER
b.1949

FIRE I
1981
Drawing and photograph
55x34

Also selected:

FIRE III
1981
Drawing and photograph
55x34

103

RICHARD DEACON
b.1949

IT'S ORPHEUS
WHEN THERE'S SINGING NO. 7
1979
Oil pastel and graphite
42x56

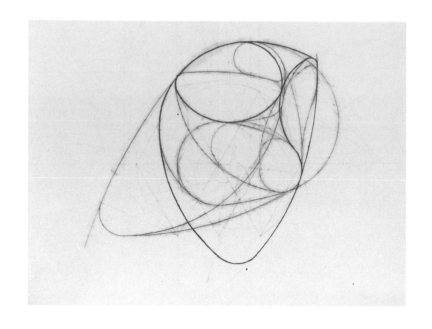

ALEX NEWCOMBE
b.1949

RESTAURANT
1977
Pencil
30x20

104

SALEEM ARIF
b.1949

DANTE'S
THE DIVINE COMEDY —
INFERNO, CANTO XXV:
VANNI FUCCI AND
MONSTER CACUS
1980-81
Watercolour and pen
11x15¼

Also selected:

DANTE'S
THE DIVINE COMEDY —
INFERNO, CANTO XVIII:
VENEDICO CACCIANEMICO
LASHED BY A HORNED DEVIL
1980-81
Watercolour and pen
11x15¼

GENEVIEVE DRAPER
b.1949

PORTRAIT OF JULIE HELD
August 1980
Pencil
22x16

DAVE BINNINGTON
b.1949

POLICE HORSE
STUDY FOR
CABLE STREET MURAL
1979
Pencil
19x12¾

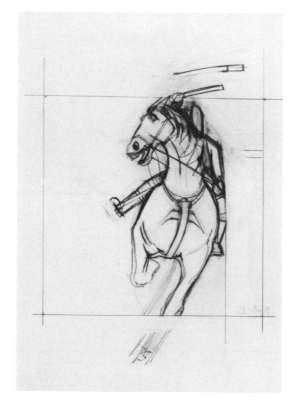

106

PAUL NICHOLLS
b.1949

HER MAJESTY'S THEATRE X
1981
Charcoal
33½ x24

JENNY-ANN FRANKLIN
b.1949

AFTER RYE, WINTER,
FEBRUARY 1982
February 1982
Mixed media
19½ x27¾

107

PAUL GOPAL-CHOWDHURY
b.1949

STUDY OF A SHY MODEL
1980
Pencil
9x6½

DAVID GRIMBLEBY
b.1949

BLACK DRAWING NO.1
1977
Coloured pencil
19x26

108

JAC ESTERHUIZEN
b.1949

PETRA TOU ROMIOU
1980
Charcoal
19½ x16

Also selected:

ROCK OF THE GREEK
1982
Charcoal
23x16½

PAUL BENJAMINS
b.1950

IT WAS JUST
ONE OF THOSE THINGS I
1982
Pastel, pencil and acrylic paint
48x60

SINEAD SIGGINS
b.1950

VIEW OF THE MOUND
1981
Pencil
5½ x 14½

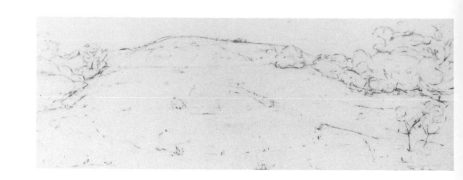

GARRY BARKER
b.1950

A DIALOGUE OF SELF
AND SOUL
(YEATS)
1982
Wax crayon, chalk and pencil
14 x 14

110

JAN WANDJA
b.1950

B & K
February 1982
Chalk
2 sections, each 69x60

 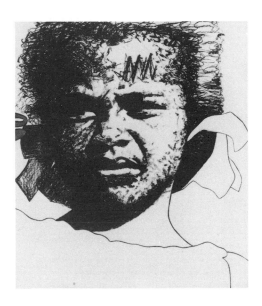

JAMES SAVAGE
b.1950

PUBLIC FIGURES
1981
Graphite
96⅛ x120½

IAN POLLOCK
b.1950

TOPLESS BARMAID
1981
Ink and ink wash
16x10

GRAHAM CROWLEY
b.1950

SANCTUARY
1981
Charcoal and pastel
40x27

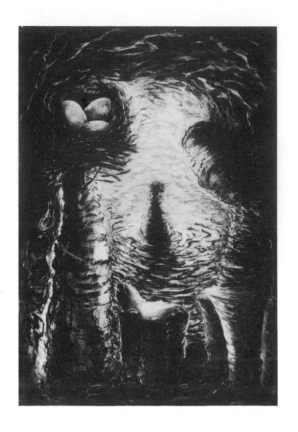

PETER RIPPON
b.1950

RAZOR STROP
November 1981
Pastel
32x40
Lent by the artist;
courtesy Nicola Jacobs Gallery

114

MOULD
1981
Charcoal and oil
23x33½

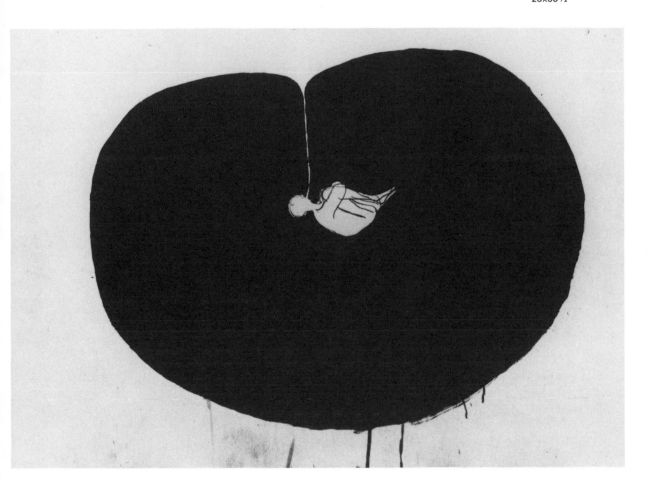

Also selected:

ART
1981
Charcoal and oil
23x33½

HOME
1981
Charcoal and oil
33½x23

JOCK McFADYEN
b.1950

AT THE BUS STOP:
THE LOVE BITE
September 1981
Pencil, ink and oil
54x40

STEPHEN FARTHING
b.1950

TILTING FURNITURE
1981
Conté and charcoal
20x28

JUNE REDFERN
b.1951

DON'T STOP 'TILL YOU GET
ENOUGH
1982
Chalk
72x48

STEPHEN COOPER
b.1951

UNTITLED
1982
Oil
33x46½

117

ROSEMARY BURTON
b.1951

HEAD OF A MAN
1981
Charcoal on canvas
48x36

SUSAN WILSON
b.1951

BY HAMMERSMITH BRIDGE
August 1981
Pencil
9¾x14½

PATRICIA HAYES
b.1951

LIFE DRAWING (1)
1981
Pencil
21 ½ x 31 ½

Also selected:

LIFE DRAWING (2)
1981
Chalk
23 ½ x 18

LIFE DRAWING (3)
1982
Coloured pencil
25 x 11 ½

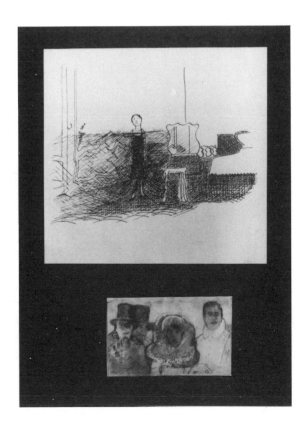

TIM FOSTER
b.1951

HE SAID HE LOVED ME
1981
Ink and pencil
16 x 13

Also selected:

AUGUST IN HOLLYWOOD
1981
Ink and pencil
16 x 13

BEN HANCOCKS
b.1951

NO.2
December 1979
Oil pastel
22½x6½

ROBERT KESSELER
b.1951

UNTITLED
1982
Pastel
20x30

120

IAN FRIEND
b.1951

UNTITLED II
1981-82
Charcoal
30x22½

JOHN EVANS
b.1951

UNTITLED
January 1982
Mixed media
33⅛ x23⅜

EDWARD ALLINGTON
b.1951

THE PRISONERS OF THE SUN
1982
Ink and emulsion
60x96

Also selected:

TOWARDS THE DEATH
OF ACHILLES
1982
Ink and emulsion
60x96

JONATHAN MILES
b.1951

UNTITLED
February - March 1982
Coloured pen
2 sections, each 40x30

DANNY LEVY
b.1952

SELF PORTRAIT IN
DRESSING TABLE MIRROR
September 1981
Conté
12x11 ¾

123

PETER McNIVEN
b.1952

HELEN IN THE BATH
AT 37 WEEKS
June 1981
Pencil
13⅝ x 12

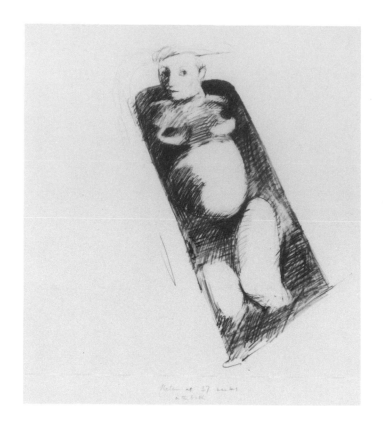

STEPHEN WEST
b.1952

FOUR STATES
November 1981
Charcoal
22x30

Also selected:

ON THE SCAFFOLDING
December 1981
Charcoal
22x15

PETER STANYER
b.1952

THE FUNERAL
1980
Pastel
51 x 41

ALAIN AYERS
b.1952

TWO BIRDS REFLECTING
January 1982
Oil, acrylic, charcoal and ink
60½ x 31½

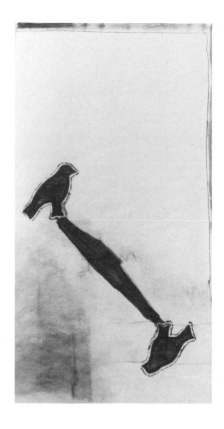

BIDDY BUNZL
b.1952

BEFORE STRAWBERRY BRONZE
1981
Acrylic
55½ x 58½

126

ANNE HOWESON
b.1952

SALE OF A VILLAGE GIRL
IN THAILAND
1981
Pastel
17x10

Also selected:

TWO PROSTITUTES AND
THEIR DOG
1980
Pastel and gouache
17x11

127

RUSSELL MILLS
b.1952

...COURAGE TO CLIMB
December 1981 -
January 1982
Graphite
25½x8½

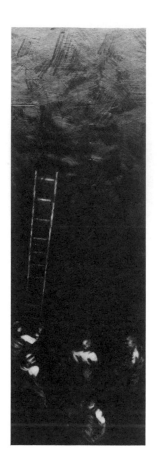

JEFF LOWE
b.1952

DRAWING FOR SCULPTURE
1982
Watercolour and pastel
14x10
Lent by the artist;
courtesy Nicola Jacobs Gallery

Also selected:

DRAWING FOR SCULPTURE
1982
Watercolour
14x10
Lent by the artist;
courtesy Nicola Jacobs Gallery

128

MAGDA KOZARZEWSKA
b.1952

PORTRAIT OF A YOUNG MAN
November 1981
Pencil
16x10¼

SIETSKE SMID
b.1952

TREE TRUNKS
1982
Charcoal
45¾x30

129

JON GROOM
b.1953

CLAY
January 1982
Oil
23x30½
Lent by the artist;
courtesy Nicola Jacobs Gallery

VANESSA JACKSON
b.1953

UNTITLED
1982
Charcoal and pastel
40x34

130

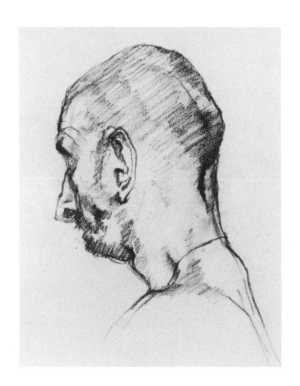

VALERIE PRICE
b.1953

KARL
June 1981
Conté
10x7

EILEEN COOPER
b.1953

HIGHER AND HIGHER
1982
Charcoal
48x36

JOHN SKINNER
b.1953

GIRL ON A LEDGE
1981
Charcoal, chalk and watercolour
23½x16½

THERESA ROBSON
b.1953

LANDSCAPE NO.1
December 1980
Pencil, ink and charcoal
14¼x19¼

132

MATTHEW RADFORD
b.1953

MY GRANDMOTHER TALKING
TO ME
January 1980
Chalk
16¾ x 16½

DAMON RAWNSLEY
b.1953

PORTRAIT
1982
Pencil and conté
23x16¼

BRUCE TIPPETT
b.1953

STUDY: KATE'S PICTURE
1982
Mixed media on museum board
18¼x43

134

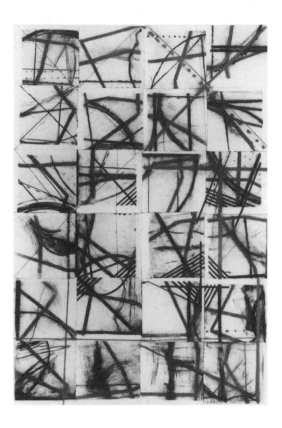

JOHATHAN GIBBS
b.1953

WINTER DRAWING
1981
Pastel and paper collage
43x29

HOWARD RAMSAY
b.1953

STUDY FOR VIEW OF
THE IRWELL VALLEY
December 1981
Watercolour and pencil
28¾x42

135

JO VOLLEY
b.1953

VIV READING
December 1981
Pencil
30¼ x 22¼

ANDREW PIESLEY
b.1953

IN TERRA PAX
10 - 20 January 1982
Pencil
8x10

Also selected:

THE FLOWERS OF THE DEAD
BLOSSOM IN TOMBS
(GAUTIER)
29 April - 15 May 1979
Pencil
11¾ x 16½

HUW MORGAN
b.1954

PENCAER
December 1981
Graphite
41½x30

CATHERINE SULLIVAN
b.1954

VILLAGE AND MOUNTAIN
ARDNAMURCHAN
1981
Watercolour
22x30

GETHIN EVANS
b.1954

FIGURE SLEEPING — NIGHT
1982
Mixed media
24½ x 27

ANDREW STAHL
b.1954

UNTITLED
1982
Pastel, pencil and ink
23½ x 30

KATHERINE VIRGILS
b.1954

FROM A SERIES OF
ELEVATION DRAWINGS
1981
Paper, paint and collage
46x42

DAVID SUFF
b.1955

WORK CONTINUES IN THE
GARDEN
1980-81
Silverpoint on gesso
20x40

MICHAEL CLARK
b.1954

MURIEL BELCHER ILL IN BED
1979
Pencil
16½ x11⅜
Private collection

CHARLOTTE VERITY
b.1954

TABLE TOP
1981
Pencil
14⅛ x20¼

Also selected:

SCISSORS
1981
Pencil
13½ x20⅜

140

PAUL FINN
b.1954

RACIAL ATTACK
January 1982
Graphite
39¾x28

EDWARD DURDEY
b.1954

FIGURE WITH TOWER
February 1982
Conté and charcoal
22x30

FIONA HENDERSON
b.1955

UNTITLED
May 1980
Collage, crayon and acrylic
29x29

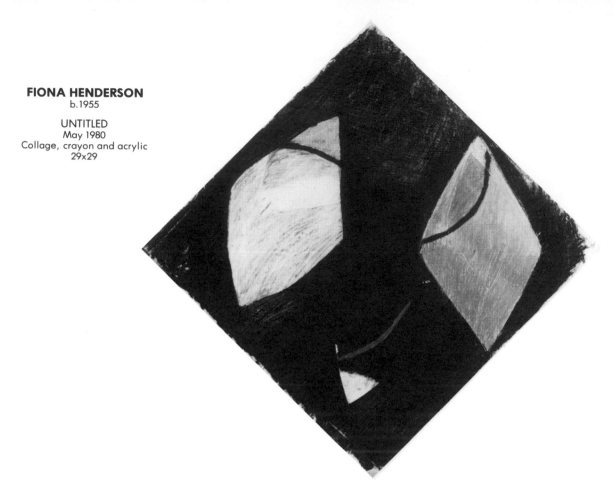

TABITHA SALMON
b.1955

SHOWCASE II: GOOSE
January 1981
Charcoal, oil pastel and gouache
23½x33

142

ANNE-MARIE FOSTER
b.1955

ONE SUMMER AFTERNOON
15 August 1980
Coloured pencil
17¾ x 16½

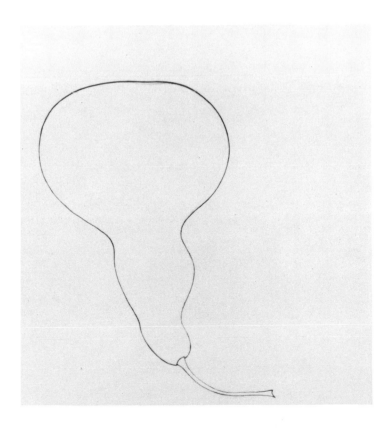

ERIC BAINBRIDGE
b.1955

GOURD
1982
Charcoal
60x55

Also selected:

TREES
1982
Charcoal
57½ x55

143

PETER FLOWERS
b.1955

SPRING BORDER
Pen, coloured ink and
coloured pencils
11x8½

MICHAEL McGUINNESS
b.1955

BUILDERS MERCHANT'S YARD,
LEYTONSTONE
1982
Charcoal
33x58

144

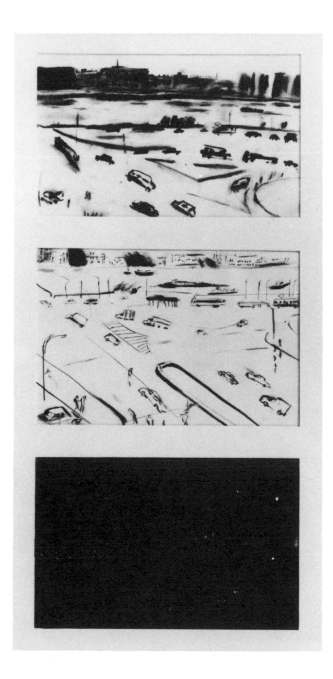

CHRISTOPHER CORR
b.1955

THE NEVA AND
ALEKSANDR NEVSKY SQUARE (1)
23 July 1981
Charcoal
5¼ x 8¼

THE NEVA AND
ALEKSANDR NEVSKY SQUARE (2)
25 July 1981
Pencil
5¾ x 8¼

THE NEVA AND
ALEKSANDR NEVSKY SQUARE,
NIGHT
24 July 1981
Pastel
5¾ x 8¼

ANNE O'RAWE
b.1955

DRAWING
1977
Pencil
26x19½

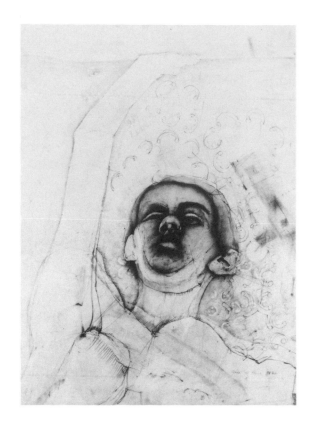

SHIRAZEH HOUSHIARY
b.1955

DUST OF TENDER GREEN
1980
Watercolour, pen and ink
24½x32

146

RACHEL SKEET
b.1955

THE ROOM, CLAPHAM
1978
Pencil
62x60

CATHERINE BLACKER
b.1955

KHUMBU HIMAL
December 1981
Map and oil paint
33x47½

Also selected:

MAHALANGUR HIMAL
January 1982
Map and oil paint
31¼x35

147

MATTHEW SHELLEY
b.1956

BASIN
1982
Pencil and pastel
22½ x 30½

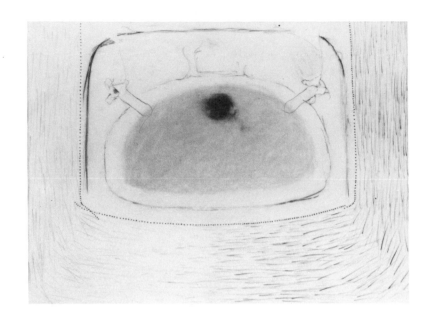

PETER CARR
b.1956

WOMAN AT A MIRROR
February 1982
Pencil
3½ x 5½

Also selected:

WORKMAN
January 1982
Pencil
6¼ x 5½

ANDREW ONISIFOROU
b.1956

SALLY SEATED
1981
Pencil
32½ x 24½

CHRISTINA BROWN
b.1956

CHRISTOPOLITISA
1979
Compressed charcoal
33½ x 46

149

ADRIAN KING
b.1956

RED FRAME
February 1982
Crayon and pencil
17½ x 14¾

JANET BELL
b.1956

BED AND CUSHIONS
1981
Charcoal
19x24

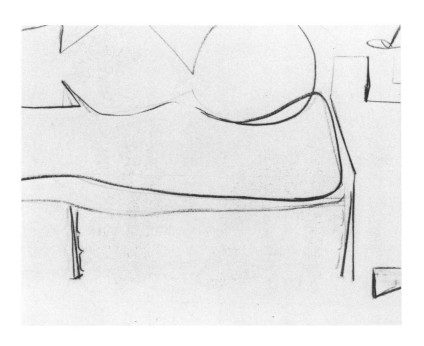

150

WILLIAM JOHN RODGERS
b.1956

FIELD DRAWING
1981
Drawing
21 ½ x 25

GRAHAM STEWART
b.1956

JIM AND TOOLS
1981
Charcoal and chalk
21x29

151

ROBERT BENNETT
b.1956

DEATH OF BRYHTNOTH
AT MALDEN
November 1981
Charcoal and pastel
51x39

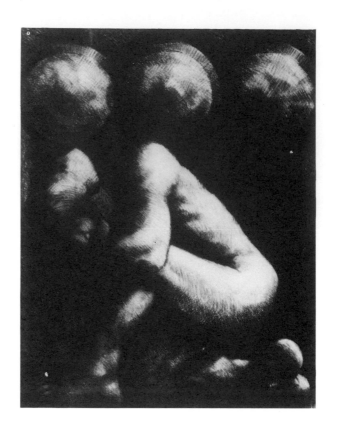

TIM LONG
b.1956

UNTITLED
1981
Graphite
20x25½

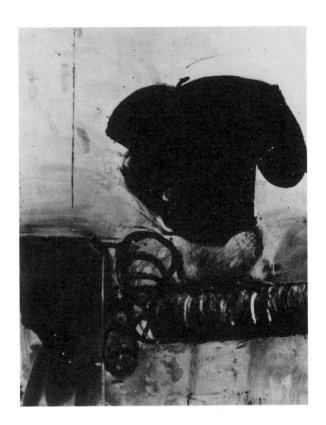

IAN PARKER
b.1956

STUDY / DOCKS FIGURE
1981
Mixed media
41½ x 31½

Also selected:

STUDY / DOCKS FIGURE
1981
Mixed media
42x32

EMMA DOUGLAS
b.1956

OVER 50's BALLROOM DANCERS
WAITING FOR RESULTS
February 1982
Graphite and oil paint
22x30

ANDREW GOLDSWORTHY
b.1956

COURTING SALMON —
BELOW MUSGRAVE BRIDGE —
RIVER EDEN
December 1981
Pencil, graphite and rubber
24x7½

Also selected:

COURTING SALMON —
BELOW MUSGRAVE BRIDGE —
RIVER EDEN
December 1981
Pencil, graphite and rubber
24x7½

COURTING SALMON —
BELOW MUSGRAVE BRIDGE —
RIVER EDEN
December 1981
Pencil, graphite and rubber
24x7½

154

LOUISE BLAIR
b.1957

IN LOVE IN PARIS
February 1982
Chalk, pencil and charcoal
50x36

MARTIN HANDFORD
b.1956

THE BATTLE OF ABOUKIR BAY
1980
Felt tip pen and
coloured pencil
14x19

Also selected:

SOD THE LOSERS
1980
Felt tip pen
8x9½

DAVID ALESWORTH
b.1957

BOATS AND VESSELS
June 1980
Crayon, chalk and linseed oil
24½ x 34

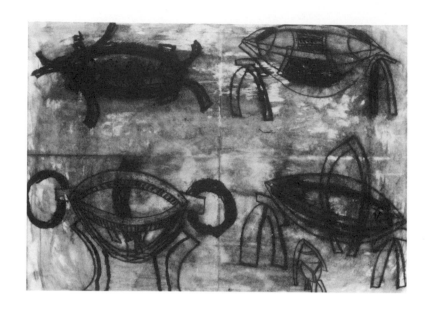

SUZANNE HUTCHINSON
b.1957

UNTITLED
1981
Conté
16½ x 23

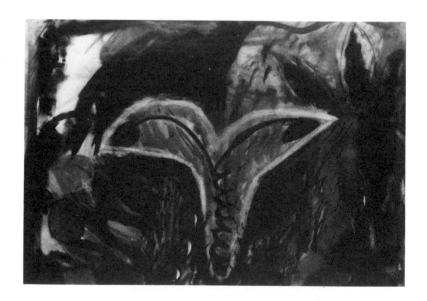

156

JILLIAN DENNIS
b.1957

HEAD OF A WOMAN
February 1981
Charcoal
27½ x 22¾

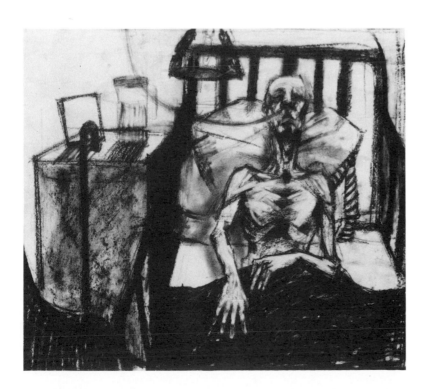

TIMOTHY POMEROY
b.1957

OLD MAN — DYING
1979
Graphite stick
20x21

157

CHRISTOPHER HOLLOWAY
b.1957

NUMB CANT
(FLOOR DRAWING)
January 1982
Pencil
24¼ x 29¼
Ilona Guinsberg

Also selected:

FLOOR DRAWING
(FIGURE STUDY)
January 1982
Pencil
20x30

JENNY WEST
b.1957

DRAWING FOR SCULPTURE
January - February 1982
Pencil and watercolour
20x28

158

LAURA KNOBLOCK
b.1957

NUDE 2
1981
Charcoal
25½x18

Also selected:

NUDE 1
1981
Charcoal
23x16½

JANE ELLIS
b.1957

JUGGLER, HORSE AND GIRL
January 1982
Charcoal
32x24½

CLARE MEADE
b.1957

OBJECTS ON TABLE
February 1982
Charcoal
30x42

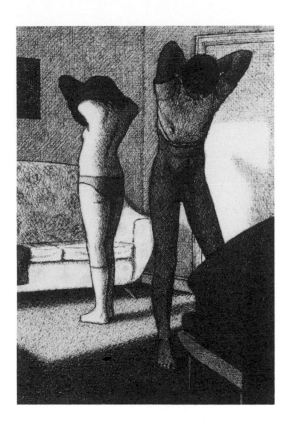

JULIAN MAY
b.1957

UNDRESSING
December 1981
Coloured pencil, pen and ink
13x9

THOMAS DEAKINS
b.1957

A STEINWAY ON HOLIDAY
May 1981
Pencil
11x14½

161

AUGUSTINE TUN
b.1957

SUBWAY FOOT
TRYPTYCH PANEL, NO.2
September 1980 - May 1981
Charcoal
49x42

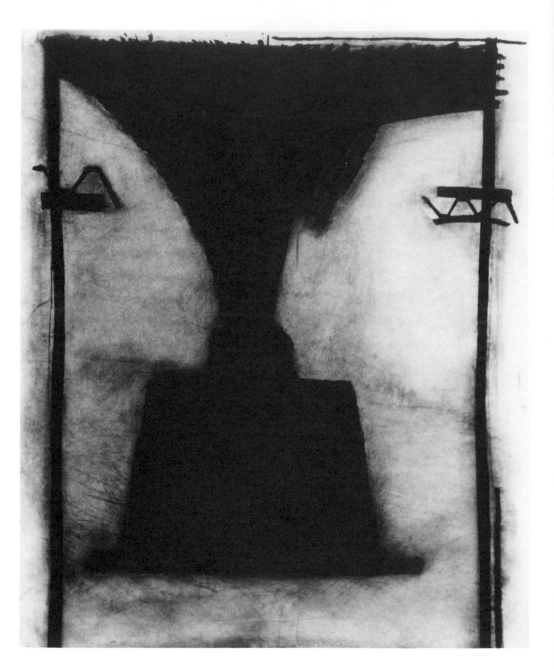

162

PETER ABRAHAMS
b.1958

SMALL NUDE
November 1981
Pencil
11 ¾ x 8

NIGEL CARR
b.1958

PROFILE STUDY OF SKULL
1981
Pencil
12 x 18 ½

BERNADETTE KERR
b.1958

SWIMMERS I
February 1981
Oil
12x9

MARK BEAVEN
b.1958

THINKING OF ENGLAND
February 1981
Crayon and charcoal
16½ x23⅜

PATRICK O'FARRELL
b.1958

PORTRAIT OF GERALD O'FARRELL
December 1979
Pencil
29x21

Also selected:

APPLE TREE
August 1980
Charcoal
28x27½

CABBAGE
1982
Pencil
18x18

SALLY FRESHWATER
b.1958

UNTITLED I
May 1981
Pencil and tracing paper
19½ x 27½

Also selected:

UNTITLED III
May 1981
Pencil and tracing paper
19½ x 27½

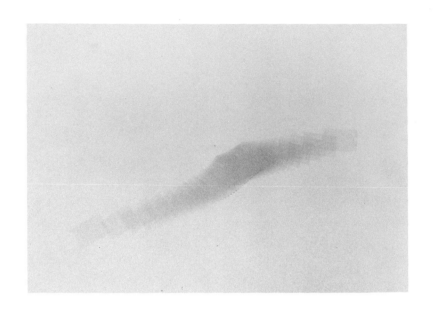

JULIE HELD
b.1958

PORTRAIT OF PETER ABRAHAMS
November 1981
Pencil
11½ x 6¼

166

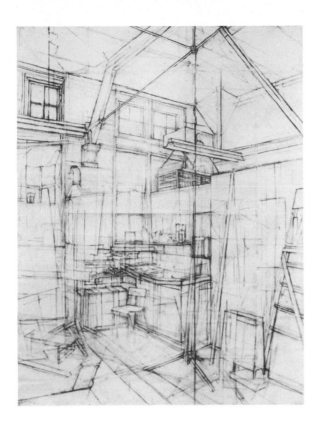

STEPHEN SCOTT
b.1958

STUDIO DRAWING I
1978
Charcoal
62x47

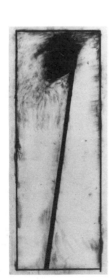

RAY WILSON
b.1958

FLAGS
October 1981
Charcoal
4 sections, each 109x42

167

JUDITH GREGSON
b.1959

SYCAMORE/ASH SEEDS
January 1982
Pencil
17x11½

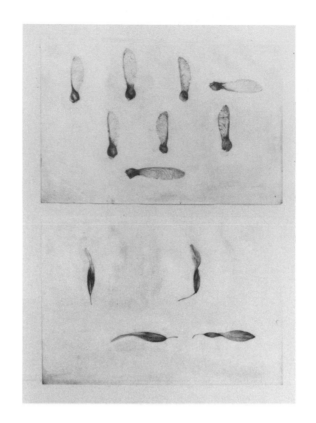

PUTRISHA LAWLOR
b.1959

MOVING OUT
January 1982
Charcoal and acrylic
34½x35

MELISSA SCOTT-MILLER
b.1959

BASKET OF FLOWERS
August 1981
Charcoal
32x23

TIMOTHY BARNETT
b.1959

GENERAL PRINCIPLES OF
TREATMENT
January — February 1982
Conté and charcoal
40x28

169

SASHA HOLZER
b.1959

THREE
January 1982
Charcoal on board
24x36

Also selected:

WORLD VIEW
12 February 1982
Pentel pen
54x40

ALASTAIR STRACHAN
b.1959

GOVAN SHIPYARDS
December 1981
Charcoal and chalk
30x21½

170

STEPHEN MASTERSON
b.1959

BELLE ET BÊTE
February 1982
Charcoal, graphite and
coloured pencil
13x16½

Also selected:

BELLE ET BÊTE
February 1982
Charcoal, pencil, watercolour,
and gouache
22x33

UNTITLED
February 1982
Charcoal, graphite and watercolour
14x18

171

SCOTT KILGOUR
b.1960

NOW WE'LL SPEND SUMMER
(STUDY 2)
February 1982
Felt pen, pencil and ink
29½ x 29½

ANITA KLEIN
b.1960

MAN WITH HEN
January 1982
Charcoal
4¼ x 6¾

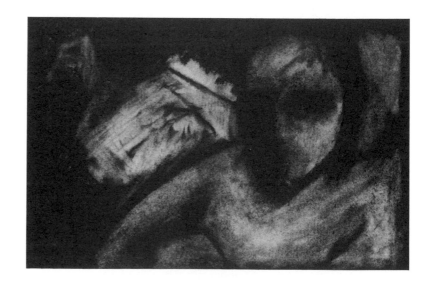

172

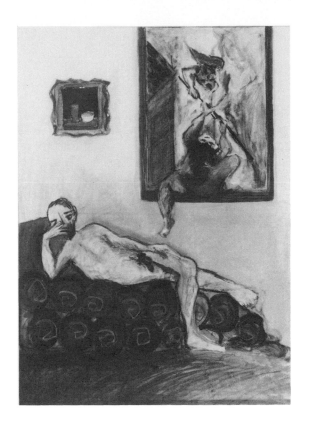

JULIA HADDON
b.1960

CASPAR AND FRIENDS
December 1981
Pastel, ink, charcoal and
poster paint
28½ x 20½

STEWART HELM
b.1960

THE BAPTISM OF CHRIST
November 1981
Watercolour on newsprint
20x30